All Scripture references taken from the KJV of the Holy Bible, unless otherwise indicated.

How to Build Houses & Dismantle Weapons

Dr. Marlene Miles

Freshwater Press 2024
Freshwaterpress9@gmail.com

ISBN: 978-1-963164-56-5

Paperback Version

Copyright 2024, Dr. Marlene Miles

All rights reserved. No part of this book may be reproduced, distributed, or transmitted by any means or in any means including photocopying, recording or other electronic or mechanical methods without prior written permission of the publisher except in the case of brief publications or critical reviews.

Table of Contents

I Built A House 4
By Wisdom... 8
Use Your Words 11
Am I Building?..17
Tearing It Down 19
God Doesn't Do Lukewarm 25
A Time to Build 33
How Long Will It Take? 42
Mind Your Breaches 49
Talkativeness...52
Spirit & Life 57
Certain Warfare 64
I Dismantled A Weapon 69
Dismantle That Weapon 74
Tear Down That House 79
Don't Build Shame 84
God Bless You 87
Praying to Build 89
Dear Reader: 92
Prayer books by this author 93
Other books by this author 96

How to Build Houses & Dismantle Weapons

I Built A House

> Wisdom hath builded her house, she hath hewn out her seven pillars:
> (Proverbs 9:1)

What did you do today? I built a house.

What?

With Wisdom, I built a house. At first, I thought it was foundation work because I had been praying fervent prayers regarding foundation. But after a time, I noticed that more than foundation was in place. It appears that in the spirit the hold up for building the house was waiting for the foundation work, which I may have been slack on or not diligent enough to complete.

In the spirit the Lord showed me massive blocks being moved and organized and placed. These blocks were thick, solid, and strong. The builders naturally knew where to place everything. As in Nehemiah, the blocks were already cut and there was no sound, there was not the sound of cutting or hammering, just the quick, silent, and efficient placement of blocks that were already the correct size and of the right material being placed correctly together that was creating an edifice that, from what I could tell yearned to be put together. It was as though if, by Wisdom and knowledge knew how to fit together, even that it may have been together in times past but something had separated chief parts that yearned to be together again.

After the foundation the building continued, and I saw the outside walls of the facade go up, the building would be at least two stories high, perhaps, three.

The blocks were huge and beautiful, almost like Jerusalem stone, beige in color with gold flecks when hit by the sunlight. This, I had seen on more than one sunrise on the roof of more than one hotel when in Israel; we were told to pray on the rooftop at every sunrise during our tour of the Holy Land.

The builders, the workers wore white or off-white linen and were not stressed or strained to move the massive blocks that would create the sure foundation and then the walls of the house.

Today I built a house.

What is a house?

A dwelling place.

A habitation for the Lord's presence. A place for meeting up and tabernacling with God.

A place for my generations. A place in God, for my generations.

It could be an actual house, but it was still in the spiritual realm, waiting to come into the physical realm.

As in our dream life, **we** are the house. So, what house did I build today? It could be any and at the same time, all of those houses. God knows and I will be informed at the right time.

By Wisdom

Wisdom has seven pillars:

The reverential fear of YHWH is the instruction of wisdom.
(Proverbs 15:23)

I capitalize Wisdom because She is a person. Also, because She is a woman who deserves both honor and respect.

The seven **pillars** of Wisdom are:

- Understanding,
- Counsel,
- Might, (strength, or fortitude)
- Knowledge,
- Power or authority,

- Riches and
- Honor.

The Spirits that are around the Throne of God are written of in Isaiah 11.

The Spirit of the LORD shall rest upon him, the Spirit of wisdom and understanding, the Spirit of counsel and might, the Spirit of knowledge and of the fear of the LORD, and He will delight in the fear of the Lord.
(Isaiah 11:2–3 NASB).

How do we attain to Wisdom? The Fear of the Lord is the *beginning* of Wisdom. First we must know that God is and have respect, reverence, awe, and fear unto Him.

The fear of the LORD is the beginning of wisdom: and the knowledge of the holy is understanding. (Proverbs 9:10)

The fear of the LORD is the beginning of knowledge: But fools despise wisdom and instruction.
(Proverbs 1:7)

The awe and reverential fear of the Lord is the beginning of both Wisdom and Knowledge.

If Wisdom builds *Her* house, then Wisdom knows how to build houses. If I have the Spirit of Wisdom can I not do the same? Can't you?

Use Your Words

Today I built a house. But how did I do it?

With my words. With my prayers.

I've heard more than one parent say to their toddler who may have been pointing to, whining or yearning for something but grunting --, *"Use your words."* By instructing us to pray and instructing us in prayer Jesus taught us to use our words. In modeling prayer and declarations and decrees, Jesus taught us to use our words. We don't just sit around moaning and complaining. We don't just rest complacently waiting for God to just do things that we want or need to have done as if He is a spiritual butler.

Some time ago I was in my doctor's office, and he instructed me to have certain blood work done. Showing him how brave I was, I rolled up my shirt sleeve and bared my arm for the drawing of blood. He laughed so hard that I had to laugh with him. Then he said, *"I don't draw blood."*

How foolish of me.

How foolish of all of us if we think God is *stepping and fetching* for us. He has angels. God's angels obey the voice of the Word of God. Therefore, it is incumbent upon us, when we use our words, to make sure we are using God's Word so the angels will come to our assistance.

> In the mouth of the foolish is a rod of pride: but the lips of the wise shall preserve them. (Proverbs 14:1-3)

So, the words that we should be speaking are full of Wisdom, Knowledge, and any attribute that is the Holy Spirit.

Having no pride also means those words should not have flesh in them, else the speaker is foolish and may fall into destruction. Wise words preserve a man and if that man is the *house*, the house the very bloodline of that man is preserved.

    Are you a builder? If you are using your words wisely, then you are. However you may find that when you use your words well, you can be a builder. Why, yes, certainly you're a builder, if you **do what you see your Father do--,** that is what Jesus said. In the beginning, God created the Heaven and the Earth by speaking. God built everything from darkness and void by speaking.

    Jesus spoke.

    Jesus did what He saw His Father do. Jesus created, healed, blessed, and even cursed that fig tree, by speaking.

    Follow me as I follow Christ. We are to follow Jesus' example and we too, *speak.*

Jesus said, ***The Words that I speak they are Spirit, and they are Life.*** We know from the Old Testament that the words of God do not fall to the ground or return void, but they accomplish what the speaker, God says they will accomplish.

We also know that the angels come to perform the Word of God that is spoken; therefore, we speak and in faith we declare, and decree and the angels come for our words, just as they did for Daniel.

A man can have whatsoever he says. Therefore, as a *speaking spirit*, as Jesus is, and as our Father, which art in Heaven. When you are speaking you are either building or tearing down something. You have the authority to create with your words; those words become spirit and also life, as Jesus spoke. And, you have the authority to tear down with those words.

Words are never neutral. Every time you or anyone speaks something happens. You may think that what is occurring is in the natural, but what is happening is in the spirit. There are 1,000 angels at our disposal so when we speak, we put them into action creating, building, or tearing down, routing out, destroying.

Which angels are you speaking to and what are you saying? Who are you to them? And, do they take you seriously and obey your commands (words)? Do you take yourself seriously?

Demons who are fallen angels spoke saying, *Jesus I know; Paul, I know, but who are you?* In other words, if you are not a serious person and if you are not known in the spirit world, you can't just waltz in and have everyone obey you. Demons behave as if you've got to earn your chops.

Sometimes, before you can build, you must first tear up or break something down. In building, to create a building that stands, a foundation is required. Digging a foundation appears that you are tearing something up – you're actually digging a hole, but in reality, you are *building*.

A lot of us think that we are building or tearing down something in the physical world, in the natural, but we are speaking spirits and the Words we speak they are Spirit, and they are Life. When we don't see an immediate effect in the physical, we think we were just playing or joking and nothing happened. Something happened; something always happens.

So, were you talking, talking, talking, even talking loud but saying nothing of value? We humans sometimes do that. It is unprofitable, but we are all sometimes guilty of it. We must use our words and make them mean something.

Am I Building?

Every wise woman buildeth her house: but the foolish plucketh it down with her hands. (Proverbs 14:1

Always, but especially when you speak, when your mouth is moving, turn on your discernment and ask the Lord, *What am I doing now? What is happening in the Spirit now when I speak thus and so? Am I building or am I tearing down?*

Am I building my life, Lord or tearing it down? Am I building my career or tearing it down? Am I building my spouse or tearing them down? Am I building my children — or am I tearing my children down?

Am I solving problems with my words or am I just talking loudly and saying nothing? Worse, am I creating problems?

As you are in Christ and you are in your right standing with God, and you are in your right position with the Lord, when you speak and also speak by faith, you are creating in the Spirit because your words become spirit and they are life. You are speaking by your powerful breath that God gave you; that breath of God breathes Spirit into your words. It breathes *life* into your words.

Just as the breath of God is breathed in to us, when we also breathe onto things, people, situations, and even into words, those words are faithful, with angelic assistance, to go out and become what we have spoken.

Your mouth, saints of God!

Do good in thy good pleasure unto Zion: build thou the walls of Jerusalem. (Psalm 51:18)

Tearing It Down

There are times when things need to be torn down. Sometimes, things need to be torn down because they should not be where they are, or they should not be *at all*. There are times where things need to be torn down in order to build the correct thing in its place. For example, evil altars had to be torn down to erect Godly altars in their place.

But you shall destroy their altars, break their sacred pillars, and cut down their wooden image.
(Exodus 34:13)

Sometimes relationships need to be broken and I'll say dismantled to put a proper relationship in place. Many mistakenly think that stopping a relationship is the end of that relationship. There are parts that linger after the relationship has stopped and continue even though two people no longer see each other, and even if there are no children between the two. Still, covenants are made, and God hates the breaking of Godly covenants. Evil covenants are made in some cases and those evil covenants must be broken, else an evil soul tie remains. By means of a soul tie any number of things can happen between two people, or happen to one person in the soul tie that they may find themselves confused or befuddled about.

The soul tie is the open door--, the door that remains open for the other party to do things to a person where they think just because they stopped seeing, dating, or sleeping with that person that everything just stopped.

Nope.

When you have sex with a person, you practically hand your whole soul to them. They can do with it as they choose. Have they also handed their soul to you? Yes.

When the relationship actively stopped; did the person give you your soul back? Did you take your soul back? Things stopped in the natural, in the physical realm, but in the spirit, depending on not just what was spoken, but what was done as to what altars were created to make that relationship what it was. Those altars are still speaking.

If what I am saying is not true, then how do people stay married? How do brother sand sisters stay as brothers and sisters all their lives? Family altars, yes. And, there are marriage altars – that's why the couple is at the altar on their wedding day. And there are relationship and situationship altars, that create soul ties and mimic Godly altars, but those altars keep things going between those people and those things that are going are usually works of the flesh through soul ties.

If you dug a well, but there was no longer water in that well, is it still a well? Yes, but with no water. It's still a hole; it is still a defect in the ground. That relationship, even it was initiated and instigated by soulish means, it has spiritual ramifications and spiritual things happened because you agreed to love So & So forever – you put the forever word on it. An altar was established – a forever altar. You stopped dating that fellow and met another, better, newer, improved person and got an upgrade. In the spirit, what has happened to that other altar?

Even though you love your new guy to the max right now and have loudly professed devotion, love, and care to him, even in the presence of family and friends, what of the other covenant? For all of your loud talking, were you even "free" to make this profession and have it mean something?

Something old needs to be torn down before something new can be built.

Something old needs to be renounced, before something new can properly start. In those times we need Wisdom to know when and HOW to do that. Blocking your old flame's number... forgotten is not forgiven. Forgotten is not forsaken. Ignored doesn't mean it is gone, especially in the spirit.

The Word sakes we are to forsake....

Hurl your lightning bolts and scatter your enemies! Shoot your arrows and confuse them!

Hurl your lightnings in every direction; shoot your arrows this way and that.

Flash [Your] lightning and scatter the foe; shoot Your arrows and rout them. (Psalms 144:6)

When it is time to destroy – Eccl 3:1 To everything there is a season, and a time to every purpose under the heaven:. A time to be born, and a time to die; a time to plant, and a time to pluck up that which is planted. There is a time to destroy. Man was put here to destroy the works of the devil.

When God created the Heaven and the Earth, He said all through Creation, *It is good. It is good.*

The devil came and corrupted Earth and mankind and everything in it that he could corrupt. The devil turned what was good into what is bad and we are here to turn it back to God's original estate.

God Doesn't Do Lukewarm

Lukewarm is for babies.

God is the Ancient of Days. He knows who He is, what He wants and how He likes things. God does not like lukewarm. He tells us to be either hot or cold, else He will spit us out of His mouth.

When you come to the Kingdom you need to be all in. Just stopping what you were doing in the world is a great start. Many are told that is all you need to do, but what of the covenants that you made when you were in the world? Have you broken them? Have you renounced the sins that caused the evil covenants to be in place? Have you properly broken up with the idols of your father's house? Have you broken up with the idol *gods* you used to serve, or do you still step out with them from time to time?

Dinah stepped out to visit the girls of the land, that is the idols of the land and got herself into a world of trouble. No, I'm not saying it was her fault, but when you are stepping out on God, who is supposed to protect you?

The idols out there and the people who worship those idols think you are out there for the same reasons that they are out there. You may call it to party and have fun, but the idols and those who serve those idols are more like the anything goes crowd and they think you are out there for that, as well.

So hot for God is easily diluted when you're also still serving idols. All of us need to be all in for God. In addition to being passionate, either hot or cold, be definitive in were you are going and why. Be all in in what you are saying at all times, especially in prayer and declarations. Devil proof your words by saying what you mean and meaning what you say.

Have you ever met someone that you just cannot understand? Are they coming or going? Are they hot or cold? Don't know, can't tell.

There's no language barrier or an accent issue, this person could be from the same country, city, town, or area as you but everything they say makes no sense to you at all. Is it because of a *spirit of confusion?* Or, is it because they don't know what they want, or are they trying to please everyone, so they are non-committal?

I had an office manager like this. I promise you, she finished zero sentences. Everything she said was just a thought and not even a complete thought. She would finish these kind of, sort of thoughts with the phrase, *"and everything else like that."*

We have no idea what she was saying, asking, implying, or trying to impart to us. Yet, she was the office manager. Looking back, it seems that the Spirits of Wisdom, Counsel, Knowledge and Understanding may not have been with her.

All of us would walk away from her meetings very confused. We know she wasn't building us up individually and we don't think she was building up the business, but it wasn't our call as she was our boss, we weren't hers.

Don't be ambivalent, don't be lukewarm, be either hot or cold, build up or tear down. Don't be wishy washy, if you're building, be bold and build. If you're tearing down, be bold and do that. Say what you mean, mean what you say.

This is spiritually significant because if you are not definitive in what you are saying, the devil, who is a legalist can meander into and weave his way into your words and turn them, twist them and torment you with your own words by bringing into manifestation and into your life things that you didn't even say--, or things you didn't believe you said, or things you didn't mean when you said the things you said.

Such as? The lyrics of secular music come to mind. You may call it just singing, but you are saying words that either are demonic or can be easily twisted to disappoint your life. How about the many songs that say that the singer doesn't need any money, just his love interest? Sing that for a decade or two and you will get just that. A thin wallet with and a relationship that is very difficult or impossible because your wallet is too thin--, flat even. Devil proof your words, even if they are the lyrics of songs. Don't be deceived into agreeing with ungodly, unscriptural words that will not benefit your life, but will diminish it.

You have to also know who you are in God. Throughout the Bible God has called and used people as prophets. The Scripture, *A man can have what he says* comes to mind, there is a prophetic grace on the words that a man speaks, especially when he believes the words that he is saying in his heart and does not doubt. That man can have what he says and that man has become like a prophet, speaking things into being.

People say be careful of what you wish for. Saints of God, be as guarded as to what you say, whether you mean it or not. This is why God tells us to stay away from foolish jesting.

One day friends and I were talking about being First Lady. To end the conversation, so I thought, I jokingly said, I'm the first lady--, I'm the first lady I see every morning when I get up and look in the mirror at my house. Sounds cute doesn't it? It's not. Sounds funny? It wasn't. The next thing I know I'm being courted by a pastor of a church, proposed to and on my way to becoming a First

Lady. That was not my intention in saying that and it was not something I was aspiring to.

Of note, several years prior a fellow had shown interest in dating me, and yes, he was a pastor of a church as well. One of the reasons I was not seeking to be first lady was this first pastor, who most ladies would think had it all together, was not someone I dated seriously, but he was one of the most controlling people I'd ever met in my life. There was no way I wanted any part of that and had grouped pastors, at large, into the category of control freaks.

Later, with that first guy, he said one day, *I dated a girl from the same town you're from and she has the same last name you have.*

I asked, *Who?*

He told me who---. Seriously--, that's my cousin, how could two people who are from the same town, with the same last name, who look JUST ALIKE not be relatives--, even sisters? People always said that that this cousin and I looked more like sisters than my own sisters, to me, and her own sisters to her. So, I had put this pastor into another category that was worse than controlling and RAN from him.

I didn't want to be First Lady of his church and was not seeking to be First Lady of anybody else's. But my own mouth betrayed me, still I was the one responsible for what came out of my mouth.

So be definitive when you speak and what you say and in what you mean. This will help you in all of your life, and especially in prayer and spiritual warfare. Do not be ambivalent or ambiguous. Build what you are building and mean it.

A Time to Build

To every thing there is a season, and a time to every purpose under the heaven: a time to be born, and a time to die; a time to plant, and a time to pluck up that which is planted;

a time to kill, and a time to heal; a time to break down, and a time to build up; a time to wee, and a time to laugh; a time to mourn, and a time to dance; a time to cast away stones, and a time to gather stones together;

a time to embrace, and time to refrain from embracing; a time to get and a time to lose; a time to keep, and a time to cast away; a time to rend, and a time to sew, a time to keep silence, and time to speak; a time to love, and a time to hate, a time of war, and a time of peace. (Ecclesiastes)

There is a time to destroy the bad things in your life, unless you want to keep suffering with them. Those on the nice side of Christianity, enjoy yourselves; I'm on the warfare side. When I read that God says to completely destroy the enemy, I believe He means it. It doesn't mean to war against flesh and blood, but against the spiritual wickedness from Ephesians 6.

If you had an infection in your body and you had to take 30 antibiotic capsules, over the course of a week, to completely destroy that infection and the agents that are causing it, wouldn't you do that? If you don't you don't kill the infection and the power that it has to make you sick or worse. If you don't, you don't destroy all the bacteria and then what's left can grow and come back with a vengeance and make you sick or worse than sick. If you don't, the bacteria may become resistant to that antibiotic and when you need that antibiotic again it is ineffective against whatever has come to infect you in the future. That is because of not completely destroying the enemy.

Why did you stop? Because you felt better? Feelings are dangerous, I keep telling you that. Feelings do not indicate what is on the ground against you, or what is in the air. Feelings is only a marker of how much whatever has affected you has affected your physical body at that time.

Did you stop because you had your own brand of unsanctioned mercy against the bacteria and you thought they were so cute and innocent and you just didn't have the heart to kill them?

People please. Take your meds and do your spiritual work so spiritual things don't come back to attack you, bite you, or kill you in the future.

God knows how much weight, pressure, and force is needed to take the enemy out. Do your spiritual work and your spiritual warfare and let God be God.

And of thy mercy cut off mine enemies, and destroy all them that afflict my soul: for I *am* thy servant. (Psalm 143:12)

Right now, we are talking about building, Nehemiah was building a wall, actually rebuilding the walls of the temple. Tobiah and Sanballat were sent to distract them from their rebuilding efforts.

Now it came to pass when Sanballat, and Tobiah, and Geshem the Arabian, and the rest of our enemies, heard that I had builded the wall, and that there was no breach left therein; (though at that time I had not set up the doors upon the gates;

That Sanballat and Geshem sent unto me, saying, Come, let us meet together in some one of the villages in the plain of Ono. But they thought to do me mischief.

And I sent messengers unto them, saying, I am doing a great work, so that I cannot come down: why should the work cease, whilst I leave it, and come down to you?

Yet they sent unto me four times after this sort; and I answered them after the same manner.

Then sent Sanballat his servant unto me in like manner the fifth time with an open letter in his hand;
(Nehemiah 6:1-5)

Folks, almost **all** of life is a distraction, that in the long-run profits little to nothing--, TV, entertainment, vacations, TikTok, petty fights among people, sibling rivalry--, they are all distractions. Fun or stressful--, they are all distractions. We believe we are focused and may say and even swear that we are not coming down off that wall, but we will continue to build. But every time life's distractions present, we turn our heads and stop looking at the work that we are doing. Each time we stop the work, Tobiah and Sanballat, the distractions sent to hinder us have just won.

The work that we are doing on the Earth involves speaking. Recall, we are speaking spirits, doing what we see Jesus do, who did what He saw Our Father, God do. We are speaking--, in our case, we are praying. All those distractions that keep us from praying and praying effectively stop the "work" that we are sent here to do and the work that we must do to be successful.

Prayer is how we do what God did by agreeing with Heaven. God could create all He created in 7 days. We won't do what God did in seven days; it may take us 100 years to build all we need to build and tear down all we need to tear down; therefore, we can't waste time with distractions, foolishness, and interruptions.

Nobody was messing with God while He was creating the Heavens and the Earth, but we have a dynamic coming at us with spiritual entities, folks, spiritual wickedness, and evil human agents bothering us *while* we are supposed to be creating and building. The enemy is erecting things in our way while we are supposed to be building things – we have to stop to tear down the evil that they have built to oppose our work, as we oppose theirs.

We do this in prayer, I reiterate.

Some religions pray 5 times a day – , some pray 3 times a day---, Oriental Orthodox Christians and others pray canonical prayers 7 times a day--- while do Western world Christians think once a day is *optional*? There is freedom in Grace, and that is wonderful if you are a grown up and mature, else Grace will do an immature person in. Use Grace as an opportunity to continue your work; pray.

Distractions can be such that you stay mad at your best friend for 3 days, or at your spouse for a week and you two stop speaking civilly to one another and neither of you is repenting or apologizing --- neither is talking to God and if you are you are talking to God about what they did to you.

People of God, you have done the worst thing ever when you have separated yourself from chief friends--, that is from true friends who may be your prayer warriors with you--, those putting 10,000 to flight, in agreement with you. Are you daft? Don't let the enemy tear down your power weapons. Not speaking to your spouse for even a moment is not smart at all--, two in a marital covenant can put some angels to flight in warfare like no others; when two become one that is an awesome weapon of war. Don't let the enemy take your power weapons out of your hands. If for no other reason, make up with your chief friends, real friends, and your spouse quickly because they are your prayer compatriots.

> How long will ye imagine mischief against a man? ye shall be slain all of you: as a bowing wall shall ye be, and as a tottering fence.

My soul, wait thou only upon God; for my expectation is from him.

He only is my rock and my salvation: he is my defence; I shall not be moved.

God hath spoken once; twice have I heard this; that power belongeth unto God. (Psalm 62:3, 5, 6,11)

How Long Will It Take?

Now that I've built this thing, this house, how long will it take to show up *in the natural*, in my real life?

If I've bult a spiritual weapon how long will it take until it works? The spiritual weapon is spiritual, it works right away because the spirit is not only faster than the flesh, it is **now**. Man wants flesh to be now, but it takes time for things in the spirit to get to the flesh. For that reason, flesh responses are delayed response while the spirit is now. Most often flesh responses and reactions are delayed because of the Mercy of God, who may be asking of us, Are you sure? Are you sure you want this--, here is a window and a way and a method to undo this before it really gets to Earth and impacts your life! The things that happen to us and around us, unless by divine intervention happen through people and men and women and other physical things and it can take time for those things to be set up so that they will happen in the Earth. That's another reason what you know just happened in the spirit, or what was told to you by the pastor, the prophet, or God Himself hasn't happened yet. Especially if it is something good, then the devil is working like the devil to block you from having it.

Therefore when you pray, speak loudly, proudly and with boldness, use the Word of God and pray your angels through so they can make what God promised you come to Earth for your benefit.

If you believe while you are praying, you receive, and it is done spiritually. Let it be done on Earth as it is in Heaven. Now, sometimes you have to put a time signature on your prayers, on your decrees and declarations and I would certainly do that. But spirit can be NOW, right now. Amen.

Depends on your faith. If you had enough faith to build it, shall you not have enough faith to believe that you have it, *as touching* and that it will manifest for you in the natural? How long will it take, really? Saints of God, how long do you want it to take? If you are the perfect sort, or believe yourself to be perfect, you will want what you have spoken into existence in the spirit to come into the natural right now, especially if it is something want like a new house, car, money, or spouse.

Sometimes it does.

Sometimes it has. Surely you can recount the goodness of God.

But if you are not sure of what you prayed for, and that you asked God correctly, or that you really want what you have asked for, your doubt can delay that thing created in the spirit from coming into the natural realm. That delay may be a blessing to you while you and God talk it out and you pray exactly what you should be praying and the right way.

This is where praying in the Spirit helps us tremendously. Sometimes we don't know what we ought to be praying for; so the Holy Spirit makes intercession. As I said, I hadn't prayed for a house; I had prayed regarding my foundation.

But God knew.

If you are not well-versed in prayer and faith – remember, you can have what you say, then what you ask God for may not be what you really want, and you may not be asking God if you are praying a soulish prayer. Perhaps God doesn't even **have** the thing you are asking Him for. An example comes to mind--, Sister Sonia's husband. Sister Sonia has Sister Sonia's husband, so God can't send that man to you. Careful of *who* you are praying to, if you make a devil deal, Satan may go out and try to get that man for you, but you will have hell to pay sooner or later, or sooner **and** later.

Maybe you've asked God for a chunk of money – if you haven't met the parameters to receive that huge sum of money by--, yesterday or whenever you believed that cash should be delivered to you, *are you even talking to God at all?* If you are asking for something ungodly, then you are not asking God; you are asking *Not-God*, or *Un-god*, which is the devil. It's okay to ask for money if you need money, but to always ask God for money, surely that gets old. Do your kids only ask you for money? There you go.

Saints of God, sometimes money is not the answer that you need, that's why God, in His Mercy will not send you money because that is not the answer that you need for the problem you have at hand. Think of multiple choice, A, B, C, or D. Using Wisdom and discernment and by the Holy Spirit if you pick the right answer for your situation, finances will come along with it. If you only pick money and ask for that, you will either still have the same problem, or worse because throwing money at issues can sometimes make things worse.

Now, *when* comes into focus: When you receive what you believe you are asking God is a condition of your faith but also of God's Mercy and His timing. As said, sometimes God gives us **time** to reconsider, rethink, or further study to show ourselves approved so we can realize what we have done in the spirit may be unscriptural, ungodly, or grievously wrong before we start dragging the cart into the natural to bring all those prayed-for *things* into our lives.

Sometimes the delay may be to build our faith. If it is impossible to please God without faith and there are several kinds and levels of faith, then Strong Faith would please God more than no faith, weak faith, or wavering faith – which might actually be doubt masquerading as faith.

Truth is, those things we've asked God for may not be goodies at all, but destructive tools and weapons that we have helped to create with our own words --- words with bad motives behind them, lust, greed, envy, jealousy, avarice, and strife. Those are the nuts and bolts that hold devil weapons together. Unforgiveness, anger, bitterness, resentment, adultery--- you know, works of the flesh.

Mind Your Breaches

But you are praying up a storm, believing that you are praying the *Will* of God, or at least the *will* of your grandma because she told you to get married by any means necessary, you're already 25, for goodness sakes! You're almost an old maid!

Or you're praying the will of your dad because he told you to get a career that allows you to earn a certain amount of money, and you are obeying Dad. In reality, you might be praying the *will* of your own *will* because you are agreeing with Grandma or dad, or your best friends.

Soulish and ungodly prayers will never build a strong fortress for your life, even though you may feel that you are building. The problem is that we have to acknowledge God and not lean to our own understanding. Our own understanding most often is only what we see right now, and does not include the vision of the future.

Getting frustrated, disappointed, or stopping the work of prayer, study and spending time with the Lord will not build your life or your protective wall either. Your wall is just sitting there. Well, worse than that your wall may not be sitting there – there are assignments against your wall to tear it down, demolish it, or at least take out some of the bricks whenever possible. So, you go back to your wall and have to start again and sometimes from a backward place.

This wall you're building will be secure; there should be no breach in your wall. However, if you stop paying attention, the enemy may not take the whole wall down, but he can make breaches in it. A breach is an access point to get to you later on, or a purchase point to dismantle that wall. You take one wall down from a building, is it still a building?

And, what of the people or the things, the property in that building, now they are exposed to be stolen from, or destroyed.

When the devil comes to attack or send in an attack, he doesn't come through the front door, all the time. There is one door in the sheepfold, but the thief doesn't use the door, he will try some other way. So, if he has left a window open or opened an access point that's how he plans to get in. While you've alarmed the door, chimed the door, wired the door, and sitting and staring at the door--, you might even have a shotgun in your lap, but the thief is on the roof or trying to get in through windows.

Talkativeness

In the multitude of words there
wanteth not sin:
But he that refraineth his lips is wise.
(Proverbs 10:1)

Talkativeness, using random words randomly will not build a house. Neither will chatting incessantly tear down evil that needs to be torn down. Often it will enhance evil. Resist the *spirit of talkativeness;* make sure you're not just talking to hear yourself talk, or running your mouth like a bad refrigerator – can't keep *nuthin'*. Instead study to be quiet, God likes a quiet and meek spirit.

Loose tongues sink ships they say. Take an alcoholic drink; the tongue is usually the first thing to loosen up. The spirits in that drink are on assignment to get information out of you. When you drink, you comply.

Let somebody put their hands on you--, especially your head, and you will probably start to talk. This could be why hairstylists and barbers know so much of their client's business. Touch could also be the why of so much pillow talk, and the revealing of so many secrets. Didn't Samson reveal the secret of his strength to Delilah, the seductress who surely plied Samson with sex?

Let no man lay hands on you suddenly.

Lay hands suddenly on no man, neither be partaker of other men's sins: keep thyself pure. (1 Timothy 5:22)

You shall give account of every word spoken –, sooner or later. Sometimes the account of what you've spoken is what you've built in the spirit. Many times the account of what we've spoken is what manifested in the natural. Saints of God, I can count too many things that I have gotten because of words that I spoke, spoke with regularity, or spoke in faith. How many people have called off work or school because of a stomachache that you didn't really have, but a few hours into that day when you wanted to just sleep because you were too tired to go to work, suddenly your stomach starts feeling weird. That stomachache is your having to give account for the words you spoke. Yes, even lies must be *accounted* for.

God knows what authority He put in you, and in teaching your hands to war and your fingers to fight, He is also teaching you to bridle your tongue by making you realize that what you speak has power. Words create and tear down. Words are weapons. If you were a policeman, or in the army, in the natural and you had a gun with so many bullets, do you not have to account for those bullets?

Words are bullets; your mouth is the gun, a real weapon.

Stayed up too late last night and just wanted to stay in and rest today? Well, you should have said that when you called your boss to say you wouldn't be in today, instead of bringing the condition of your stomach into the matter. Ask yourself this, would you rather be a liar or have the stomachache that you prophesied over yourself?

Our God is merciful. Angels of God were wondering when you spoke WHY in the world would you want a stomachache; but you prophesied a stomachache. Hey--, at least you're not a liar *(this time)*.

We still have to give account for every word we speak, but wouldn't it, shouldn't it be better to have the fruit of your words show up in the spirit and then in the natural and let those works speak for you? God is merciful. With discernment you can see into the spirit and see what's there or what's coming down the pike and **deal** with it before it manifests in the natural and bowls you over like ten pins in an alley. Folks, some of what is in the spirit waiting to accost you, you created. Some things are words from the imagination of others that they have created, and if you have either no walls or breaches in your walls, those evil imaginations can get into your life.

> For a dream cometh through the multitude of business; and a fool's voice is known by multitude of words.
> (Ecclesiastes 5:3)

Don't be too chatty in prayers; make sure you get to the point. Regarding prayer points, I use them myself, because they are proven to be effective by others. You don't need to reinvent things that work. However, you can tweak a prayer point to make it thorough enough to cover what you are praying for and about.

Spirit & Life

The Words you speak are **spirit and they are life** – now that you've built something in the Spirit – *now what?*

It must and will come into manifestation in the natural, sooner or later--, well, eventually– depending on your faith. Pray it *through,* if it's good. Pray it away, dismantle it and forbid it from coming to you if it is bad.

Pay close attention here: When I built that house at the beginning of this book it was not because I had asked God for a house. Whether it was a future house for myself, or whether I was building a place of meetings for me and the Lord, or building up my person, or even a place for my generations that will come after me, I was building a house. I had not asked God for a house, but the Lord knows the things we have need of. Further, the blessings of God maketh rich and He adds no sorrow.

God has made provision for us, He has given us precious promises that are automatically ours if we are in right standing with Him. I am saying that by your right relationship with the Lord, by your right standing in Him and your prayer life and proper use of everything He has given you, even spiritual weapons, God will bless you, automatically. He answers yes, and amen to your prayers; He really does.

If what you've created in the spiritual realm is bad, then here comes a crop that you may be ashamed of, unless in that waiting period you renounce what is coming to you. Warfare is to keep it out of your life --- and out of your children's lives… when you pray to renounce, denounce and undo some of the stuff you've created in the spirit, you must consider time and space because Spirit is **outside** of time.

If what you built doesn't come into manifestation in the natural world in your lifetime, it's waiting for your kids, unless you undo it, repent for it, dismantle it.

When people are about to transition from the Earth realm, they often want to see folks and maybe confess things or ask for forgiveness of people. That's well and good, but deathbed repentance is profitable for your children and your *children's* children. Talk to God. Even in the eleventh hour, repenting and renouncing and breaking evil covenants and curses is a gift you should give your family if there is time and space for such a thing.

Use your words to bless your generations, not just speaking a blessing over each one as the patriarchs of the Bible often did, but building and speaking blessings over your entire bloodline for their entire lives..

Saints of God might we all be shockingly surprised to find out who we are in the spirit. To find out what we are doing in the spirit, especially at night while we are asleep. To find out who we know, who we are with, how we go there, what we do there. What if a person finds out that they go to the coven at night, unbeknownst to them? What if they find out that they've been initiated, like--, years ago? Look if you've been initiated, you've been initiated.

Some will be shocked to find out that they have an entire spirit family--, husband kids, the whole thing.

None of this is cool with God. None of this is of God. These are the things that you must undo if you've been duped or lulled into occultic or witchcraft sin in your lifetime. Renounce and denounce it, and turn to Christ, now.

But when spiritual things manifest in the natural, and they eventually will—take a look at that verse, what is done in darkness will come to the light. What is done in the darkness, in your dream state will eventually be known to you in the daylight. Said another way, what is done while you are not aware is in darkness to you, but when you become aware of it, it is as though the Light of God, the Light of Truth shines on it and becomes visible, discernable, evident. And, amen.

Amazing Grace is the opposite of magic! Magic is now you see it, now you don't. God by His Amazing Grace is: Now you see it—when it used to be that you didn't.

Because you didn't see it, some of you who have been blindsided by *what*? How did *that* happen? What did I do to deserve this? Sometimes nothing. Sometimes everything. You could be having your entire spirit life at night doing whatever with no awareness, or with knowledge thinking it's just a dream, just a vision, that it's not important.

Dreams are important, they inform you as to who you are and they are in place to help you know what to pray about so when these things manifest in the natural, you are not shocked!

Still, you may have done nothing to bring unpleasant things into your life. Your ancestors built something negative with their words and actions, and that *thing* sat out in there in the spirit until it could locate your bloodline again. If this particular thing that is associated with your bloodline is tied to a certain age that the people get to in your father's house -- it suddenly hits you! It has found you!

That person in your bloodline should have been building a blessing for himself, herself, their children and their *children's* children, but it turned out to be a weapon that could be used against your or your family. Perhaps they were duped and thought they were protecting themselves or their bloodline and ended up being cursed. Not knowing that anything untoward had happened, they did nothing else but live the life they thought they had created that would bless them.

Your ancestor may have died and then all that was deposited in your family's foundation and left for the next generation. Sometime later you came along as one of those *generations* of your bloodline and without prayer, discernment, spiritual covering, Wisdom and her seven pillars, and a wall without breaches, you may have been blindsided by what was out there in the spirit waiting to get to you.

Certain Warfare

    This is where certain warfare must come into play because some of what is "out there" was sent to you by household witches, polygamous adversaries, evil associates' witchcraft, exes, general haters, witches, warlocks, blind witches and intentional occultic people who may be evil human agents targeting you specifically, or in need of a victim or candidate to either save their own life or get promoted in the ranks of darkness.

    We pray and we seek the Lord, so we are not suddenly attacked by the above sort – but they are out there.

    Again, who you are--, who you really, really are critical and you must know who you are and become what and who you are supposed to be in the LORD if you want to survive and prosper in this life. In your purpose and in your protection is your destiny.

If you have found out that you go to the coven at night by discernment or revelations in your dream life, you have a lot of spiritual work to do, else you will be building some terrible weapons against yourself and your generations, as well as doing harm to others in the now. If you've been initiated you have to renounce witchcraft, like yesterday. Did it come down your family line, or is it something you have done to cause this?

Thank God that you are not a witch or warlock, but when spiritual things manifest in the natural, and they eventually will, will those things be good things that you've built? Or, will they be negative things that you have either helped to fashion against yourself? Will they be things that have been sent against you that you've either not discerned, or may have known were out there but did nothing about? Is what is out there in the spirit sent to you by any of the types listed at the beginning of this chapter? If so, they have formed weapons that you have to take down before those weapons take you out.

Don't wait to be blindsided and find yourself exclaiming, *What! How did that happen?*

Dreams are important, they are the preview into your life so you can handle things in the spirit before they come to the natural where they are usually so much harder to deal with. Dreams are a preview so when these things manifest in the natural, you are not shocked, but instead, prepared.

Have you ever seen a bug near a window or somewhere in your house but it was dead? There could be any number of reasons why, but look at that as a spiritual problem that was trying, trying, trying to work itself into your environment. It didn't come in by the door, but by some other opening. But you prayed, right? You were prayerful. You may not have known exactly what was happening, but you knew something was, so you had been praying. You actually stay prayed up, right? Amen. Because of your prayer life, by the time that spiritual thing (insect) worked its way into your life (house), it was already dead.

Why is it there? It has to be there. Why didn't it die on the outside before it came into your house? Because it is a dead weapon, a failed weapon on a failed assignment--, it has to show itself to you, mighty prayer warrior. It has to show itself, it must show itself so you can know of the victory.

Whether this "bug" was created by you, was an evil gift from down your bloodline, or sent to you by an evil human agent or a result of your own sin it still formed. Now if you caused it or became aware of it and you quickly fell under conviction by the Holy Spirit, and repented, it still was defeated and had to show itself.

Ewww! It's a bug and it's in your house, but it had to show itself.

I Dismantled A Weapon

Ever see a guy, like a soldier or a hired hitman in a movie take apart a gun in no time flat? *No weapon formed against you shall prosper* – that is if you are **in** Christ. But listen saints of God, the weapon will form but it won't prosper.

God can do that too. God can take apart a weapon in no time flat.

Jesus could do it. When He healed folks that were on their cooling boards, on their death beds or walking dead, He dismantled weapons diligently assembled and fashioned by the devil to take them out, and bring them to hell. Yeah, the devil likes collecting souls, as if people are a Pokémon or baseball cards to be collected.

The devil wants one then the other, then the other. He wants all. The devil wants to take God's people from God.

But my Bible says that nothing can take me out of God's hands.

That hasn't stopped the devil from fashioning custom-made weapons against folks, saved and unsaved, to try to take them out.

> No weapon that is formed against thee shall prosper; and every tongue that shall rise against thee in judgment thou shalt condemn. This is the heritage of the servants of the LORD, and their righteousness is of me, saith the LORD. (Isaiah 54:17)

It will form and you will **see** it – that is by God's great Mercy because He wants to teach you. It was formed; it did form. **Look at it**, God may be saying.

This is a study of the enemy's weapons – weapons in general, or weapons against you. You have to know the enemy's weapons so you can recognize if this thing is coming at you again. And/or you can help another who is going through this. You are a soldier in the Army of the Lord, *right*? Then you have to know weapons.

Look at this weapon. Look at that one. Some don't want to look, it's too scary, or I *don't* know *nuthin'* about weapons, or if it's not going to hurt me now, why do I care? Let's go on with life.

God says, **Look at this**, but I will disable it, deprogram it, dismantle it and keep it from hurting you. God may be showing you a weapon that was fashioned against you and telling you that He has already disabled it, deprogrammed it, or dismantled it. If you are in Christ and you have opened your mouth to counter the effects of that particular weapon, God may be showing you what you have done in the spirit by prayers--, by your words.

As God looked on His works in Creation, should you not look over your works and see what you have created and declare, *It is good*, just as your Father did. We have that authority, you know. And, shouldn't you look over the damaged, dismantled weapons that have failed against you and also say, *It is good?*

God did not say the weapon wouldn't form. The forming of that weapon and God allowing you to see it gives you information into the spiritual mapping of your family's spiritual issues and informs you as to how to pray and what to pray for.

It also gives you an opportunity to celebrate the Lord so you can see what He has brought you through and out of – Hallelujah.

and every tongue that shall rise against thee in judgment thou shalt condemn,
(Isaiah 54:17)

Every tongue that rises up against you: That's people in the natural saying bad stuff about you. And that is also people enchanting in the spirit – their evil imaginations, gossip and what they think is going on with you, and what they **want** to be going on against you.

All that is tongues wagging --- you shall **condemn** them and how do you do that? With your own words in spiritual warfare.

Saints of God, look at the weapon, even though it may be dead right now. Take a good look, because the *next* time God may not dismantle it for you. The angels may not dismantle it for you. The next time, you may need to know how to do it yourself, for yourself, or for another person, that you know, love, or care for. Yes, by help of the Holy Spirit, but you still have responsibility to learn and do what you came to Earth to learn and do.

Dismantle That Weapon

This is all providing that you are in Christ and prayerful, praying, opening your mouth and praying the Word of God, because until and unless the Holy Spirit tells you what's out there waiting to attack you – you don't know.

So, keep on saying, *no weapon formed* because surely there must be weapons that are formed. Don't take part in the forming of weapons against you by saying ungodly things trying to sound clever or cute, talking loud and saying nothing of value.

Be sure that when you are talking, sharing, speaking, or praying that you are saying positive, valuable, godly things ---

because you are either building or tearing down something with those words. Those words are spirit and they are life. Devil proof your words, make sure they can't be turned or twisted into weapons for the devil's use against you.

By the time you see a weapon that has been formed against you is it at the onset? Is it after the weapon has already been fired at you – and missed? Or is it after the weapon has gone limp and cannot perform against you – God is just showing you one of their crafty devices that could not work against you.

He disappointeth the devices of the crafty, so that their hands cannot perform *their* enterprise.

He taketh the wise in their own craftiness: and the counsel of the froward is carried headlong.

They meet with darkness in the daytime, and grope in the noonday as in the night. (Job 5:12-14)

Dismantle that weapon while it is still in the spirit because it will take exponentially more work to fix the problems from a weapon that detonates against you in the natural. Shrapnel goes everywhere and you can't say where or how much damage there will be.

Regarding sin, quickly dismantle a weapon formed because of your own sin---, repent quickly. Renounce sin. Denounce sin. Break evil covenants formed by sin and break every curse that is allowed because of the evil covenant. Then bind and paralyze the demons assigned to enforce the curse. If the cause has been long-standing and involves others, especially family members and there is collective captivity, break all of that as well as the bondages and yokes of sin.

Do you see that what is involved to get rid of this problem is far more complicated than you may have thought? Dismantle, deprogram, and shatter bondages, yokes and the like. Saints of God, it can be more complicated than this, but you see that it is easier to not be careless and foolish with words, speaking things that do not matter that can come back and bite you or form weapons that the devil can shoot at you.

- Every evil arrow, back to sender, in the Name of Jesus.

FYI, at last count it is said that there are two main evil arrows, arrows of affliction and arrows of death. However, subcategories under either affliction or death count more than 70 named evil arrows. How much time do you think it will take you to send back 70 evil arrows? Specifically, how much time do you think you will lose off building your Wall if you are constantly on the defensive – yes, in prayer, but on the defensive sending back evil arrows?

Sometimes the weapon **is** to keep you so busy that you aren't eating right, studying right, sleeping right, praying right, or at all, worshipping, --, sometimes that **is** the weapon.

You do see how this is nothing to play with, *right?*

Tear Down That House

A curse is like a beehive full of angry bees. It's a hornet's nest full of monster hornets. You may not be allergic to them, they may not sting you, but they will surely try.

I have to insert this here: Have you ever had a person to try to lead you into a curse? Try to lead you into agreeing with a curse and it's not even true, but they want you to agree with them on something against you and you won't, so the struggle is for them to twist those words another way to get you to agree with them. **DON'T DO IT.** Listen intently on what you are hearing, what is being said, what is being spoken and don't agree with everything a person says – I don't care who that person is.

Do not agree with the curses and evil imaginations of others who are talking loudly and saying nothing.

Agreeing with the words of others is a form of prayer; it is a prayer of agreement, where the other person may have spoken the words--, that is said the entire "prayer" but then you either foolishly agreed with their prayer, not discerning it that prayer was evil, against you, ungodly, or not.

Even at church, what comes to mind is anything from what the preacher is preaching from the pulpit, to what the prayer warrior is asking you to agree with, to the words that the choir is singing. Now, this is my own personal issue that I've had for years, but it is one of the reasons why I used to be in choirs, but I am not right now. It is because some of the words to songs that may be very beautiful and also popular, my spirit man or the

Holy Spirit, as I hear and feel the Holy Spirit does not believe certain words. If I am in that choir, I am then directed to sing words that I may consider words of unbelief or doubt. So, I stepped down from choirs. That's me.

Prayer points. I am very discerning about what I say, how I say it, and what is said that I should agree with. That's me.

Some preachers are very entertaining and charismatic. Some people are the same and they are not even preachers. There is a fellow with a seducing spirit. He either doesn't realize that he has a seducing spirit, or he may not think that others realize it, but he has a way of getting his way with people. Do you fall prey to that spirit since it is not of God? Do I? No, we must guard ourselves against any spirit that is not of God. I've met more than one pastor who has that *spirit* working in them, so of course I will not agree with everything anyone says, a relative, a friend, or anyone in any place at any time.

Yes most all of us work by encouragement, we all want to be celebrated and not just tolerated. Further a preacher may do better if he knows he's on the right track with his message by the congregation's amens. This is not a pep rally folks, it's the Word of God and Jesus must be preached, and Him crucified. Is that what is happening? Well good, go ahead with the Amen's.

A prophet gets up; is every word out of that prophet's mouth *of God*? Someone gives a Word of Knowledge, is it of God? You must know before you agree with it. Someone speaks in tongues and someone else who has discernment says what it means. Does that jibe with your spirit? Is the Holy Spirit telling you, yes, good, that is right? Or is the Holy Spirit indicating something else to you?

Discern every *spirit*, weigh out what you hear, especially before you amen it, or agree to it. Those are prayers and when you agree, they become prayers of agreement.

When evil is sent your way and you do nothing about it, but just wait and see, or say something like, God has got this, you *haven't done nuthin'*, you have agreed with the evil that has been sent to you. Folks, if you found a bird's nest in an inconvenient place at your house and left it there, then you agree with the bird family--, they can do as they please on your property. So, you can agree by agreeing verbally or non-verbally. You can agree by your actions--, by going along with the program and helping out, or by not refusing the program. Those are four ways of agreement, but they are agreement.

Don't Build Shame

Whenever you are talking, especially when talking to God or making declarations against darkness make sure that you are making sense, not just talking to be talking, talking loud and saying nothing. Put some respect on those words, put value on those words that you are privileged to speak by your authority in Christ.

You are in Christ; you are representing the Kingdom. The words you speak are like apples of gold in pictures of silver. Would you rather speak that or some random slang that will either do nothing in the world or for the world, or end up being some type of harvest that you'll be ashamed of and have to give account for and answer to God about later?

What fruit did you have then in the things of which you are now ashamed? For the end of those things *is* death. (Romans 6:21 NKJV)

If your mouth is moving, make sure you are aware that your words are Spirit, they are life, they have impact and they ca have longevity.

A man can have what he says.

Death and life are in the power of the tongue: and they that love it shall eat the fruit thereof.
(Proverbs 18:21)

Saints of God, you have the unique ability to speak death and life at the same time. Death to the things of darkness and LIFE to the things of your life as you Bless the Lord.

The words you speak in your house will build it or tear it down. Choose to build it.

Today I built a house. and if you are in Christ, so can you.

God Bless You

Wisdom hath builded her house, she hath hewn out her seven pillars:
(Proverbs 9:1)

What did you do today?

Today, I built a house. It is most likely and most probable that I was able to build a house today because the day or the days before I built or started to build, I tore down something. I dismantled something, I tore down something, I tore up something that wasn't supposed to be there, that wasn't supposed to be built up in my life or in my environment.

This may mean that today or some other day I dismantled a weapon. Both these things, the building and the tearing down, the taking down and the dismantling of spiritual weapons were both done in the spirit, in prayer, in agreement, or disagreement by decrees, renouncement, denouncement and declarations, but all in the spirit.

Physical things cannot solve spiritual problems, but the spirit can trump the natural and that is most often what we are asking God and His Heavenly Host to do--, intervene spiritually, divinely on our behalf and correct and perfect those matters that concern us.

Praying to Build

Full disclosure, in all this building, I was praying in the Spirit. But before that I had been praying that previous week for about 21 non-consecutive hours about my foundation. At that time, I was praying in the Spirit only when I saw the foundation being built or restored, when I saw the walls of the house coming up, when I saw the house being built. I am under a prophetic Grace so I can speak and decree and declare a thing and it shall be. But God used folks all through the Bible as prophets.

So, whether you pray with the understanding, in the Spirit, or both, your prayers to God shall be effective. And, no matter what your Spiritual gifting is or the administration of that gift, whatever you are anointed and appointed to do, that you shall do. You shall do it if you are diligent and fervent in prayer because in that wise you shall become what God has called you to become. And once you become the what and the who you are supposed to be in the Lord, He cannot resist you. The blessings from Heaven will flow automatically.

Perhaps you are a prayer warrior, and you are very anointed to build spiritual weapons by your utterances. Perhaps you build buildings, houses, or set captives free. Perhaps you dismantle demonic booby traps and bombs. Perhaps you intercede for others and win souls. Whatever you do, you must do it; if you have the gifting you must use it. Sure, watch your football or soccer game, there is time for relaxation and/or entertainment, but if you are going to be speaking loudly, then use that volume and passion to decree and declare. Shout against the enemies of God to scare them out of their hiding places. Don't just talk loud and say nothing of any meaning, importance or value.

While praying in the Spirit, when this *house* was being built, I was home alone. You may be one to minister in a group or even to a whole congregation. Every word, every breath from your being is either building or tearing something down. Be sure you are tearing down the works of the enemy and building people, building purpose, building destiny for yourself, your family, and the people of God.

Dear Reader:

Thank you for acquiring and reading this book. I pray it has been a blessing to you and will change how you see and do things, spiritually, for the better.

In the Name of Jesus,

AMEN.

Dr. Marlene Miles

Prayer books by this author

While most books by this author have prayer points either throughout the book or at the end, there are some books that are only prayers. You just open up the book and pray. They are listed below:

Prayers Against Barrenness: *For Success in Business and Life*

Fruit of the Womb: *Prayers Against Barrenness*

Beauty Curses, *Warfare Prayers Against*
https://a.co/d/5Xlc20M

Courts of Marriage: Prayers for Marriage in the Courts of Heaven
(prayerbook) https://a.co/d/cNAdgAq

Courtroom Warfare @ Midnight
(prayerbook) https://a.co/d/5fc7Qdp

Demonic Cobwebs *(prayerbook)*
https://a.co/d/fp9Oa2H

Every Evil Bird https://a.co/d/hF1kh1O

Gates of Thanksgiving

Spirits of Death, Hell & the Grave, Pass Over Me and My House

Throne of Grace: Courtroom Prayer

https://a.co/d/fNMxcM9

Warfare Prayer Against Poverty
https://a.co/d/bZ611Yu

Other books by this author

AK: The Adventures of the Agape Kid

AMONG SOME THIEVES

Ancestral Powers https://a.co/d/9prTyFf

Backstabbers https://a.co/d/gi8iBxf

Barrenness, *Prayers Against* https://a.co/d/feUltIs

Battlefield of Marriage, *The*

Blindsided: *Has the Old Man Bewitched You?* https://a.co/d/5O2fLLR

Break Free from Collective Captivity

Casting Down Imaginations

Churchzilla, The Wanna-Be, Supposed-to-be Bride of Christ

Curses of Blind Men

Demonic Cobwebs (prayerbook)

Demonic Time Bombs

Demons Hate Questions

Devil Loves Trauma, *The*

Devil Weapons: Unforgiveness, Bitterness,...

The Devourers: Thieves of Darkness 2

Do Not Swear by the Moon

Don't Refuse Me, Lord (4 book series) https://a.co/d/idP34LG

Dream Defilement

The Emptiers: *Thieves of Darkness, 1*
https://a.co/d/5I4n5mc

Evil Touch

Failed Assignment

Fantasy Spirit Spouse
https://a.co/d/hW7oYbX

FAT Demons (The): *Breaking Demonic Curses*

The Fold (5-book series)

- The Fold (Book 1)
- Name Your Seed (Book 2)
- The Poor Attitudes of Money (3)
- Do Not Orphan Your Seed (4)
- For the Sake of the Gospel (5)
- My Sowing Journal

Gang Ups: Touch Not God's Anointed

got HEALING? Verses for Life

got LOVE? Verses for Life

got HOPE? Verses for Life

got money? https://a.co/d/g2av41N

How to Dental Assist

How to Dental Assist2: Be Productive, Not Wasteful

I Take It Back

Legacy

Let Me Have A Dollar's Worth
https://a.co/d/h8F8XgE

Level the Playing Field

Living for the NOW of God

Lose My Location
https://a.co/d/crD6mV9

Man Safari, *The*

Marriage Ed. Rules of Engagement & Marriage

Made Perfect in Love

Money Hunters: Beware of Those

Money on the Altar https://a.co/d/4EqJ2Nr

Mulberry Tree https://a.co/d/9nR9rRb

Motherboard (The) - *Soul Prosperity Series*

Name Your Seed

Occupy: *Until I Return*

Plantation Souls

Players Gonna Play

Power Money: Nine Times the Tithe

https://a.co/d/gRt41gy

The Power of Wealth *(forthcoming)*

Powers Above

The Robe, Part 1, The Lessons of Joseph

The Robe, Part II, The Lessons of Joseph

Seasons of Grief

Seasons of Waiting

Seasons of War

Second Marriage, Third--, *Any Marriage*

https://a.co/d/6m6GN4N

Sift You Like Wheat

Six Men Short: What Has Happened to all the Men?

Soul Prosperity soul prosperity series 3
https://a.co/d/5p8YvCN

Souls Captivity soul prosperity series 2

The Spirit of Poverty

StarStruck

SUNBLOCK

The Swallowers: *Thieves of Darkness*, 3

Take It Back

This Is NOT That: How to Keep Demons from Coming at You

Time Is of the Essence

Too Many Wives: *Why You Have Lady Problems*

Tormenting Spirits   https://a.co/d/dAogEJf

Toxic Souls

Triangular Power *(series)*

- Powers Above
- SUNBLOCK
- Do Not Swear by the Moon
- STARSTRUCK

Uncontested Doom

Unguarded Hours, *The*

Unseen Life, *The* (forthcoming)

Upgrade: How to Get Out of Survival Mode

- Toxic Souls (Book 2 of series)
- Legacy (Book 3 of series)

The Wasters: *Thieves of Darkness*, Bk 2
https://a.co/d/bUvI9Jo

What Have You to Declare? What Do You Have With You from Where You've Been?

When I Was A Child, *I Prayed As a Child*

When the Devourer is Rebuked

https://a.co/d/1HVv8oq

The Wilderness Romance *(series)* This series is about conducting a Godly relationship and marriage with someone who is a Wilderness person. It is about how to recognize it and navigate through it. These books are about how not to get caught up in such.

- *The Social Wilderness*
- *The Sexual Wilderness*
- *The Spiritual Wilderness*

Other Series

The Fold (a series on Godly finances)
https://a.co/d/4hz3unj

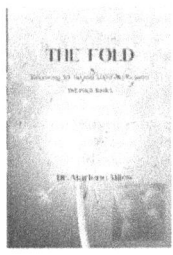  

Soul Prosperity Series https://a.co/d/bz2M42q

Spirit Spouse books

https://a.co/d/9VehDSo

https://a.co/d/97sKOwm

Thieves of Darkness series

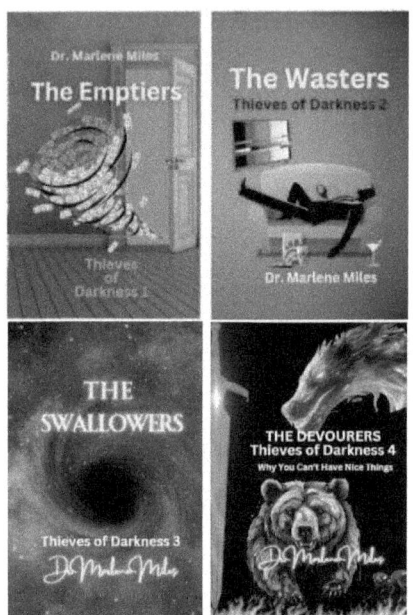

Triangular Powers https://a.co/d/aUCjAWC

Upgrade (series) *How to Get Out of Survival Mode* https://a.co/d/aTERhX0

www.ingramcontent.com/pod-product-compliance
Lightning Source LLC
Chambersburg PA
CBHW060845050426
42453CB00008B/836